Welcome to India

By Patrick Ryan

The Child's World®

Welcome to the WORLD

Published by The Child's World®
1980 Lookout Drive
Mankato, MN 56003-1705
800-599-READ
www.childsworld.com

Content Adviser: Vinay Lal, Ph.D., Associate Professor, History Department,
University of California Los Angeles (UCLA), Los Angeles, CA
Design and Production: The Creative Spark, San Juan Capistrano, CA
Editorial: Publisher's Diner, Wendy Mead, Greenwich, CT
Photo Research: Deborah Goodsite, Califon, NJ

Cover and title page: Steve Vidler/SuperStock
Interior photos: Alamy: 3,16 (Marryam Reshii/Indiapicture), 13 (Dinodia Images), 20 left (Keren
Su/China Span); Animals Animals Enterprises: 6 (Khalid Ghani); CORBIS: 12 (Bettmann), 24
(Richard Powers), 25 (Catherine Karnow); Dreamstime.com: 7 top (Paul Prescott), 8 (Mike Rogal);
Getty Images: 14 (Karan Kapoor), 3, 15 (Peter Adams/Taxi); iStockphoto.com: 21 (Dario Diament),
23 (Alan Chao), 28 (Ufuk Zivana), 29 (Hendrik De Bruyne), 30 (Minnie Menon), 31 (Rebecca Picard);
Landov: 9 (Beate Schleep/dpa), 20 right (Jagadeesh/Reuters), 22 (Arindam Mukherjee), 27 (Ajay
Verma/Reuters); Lonely Planet Images: 7 bottom (Sara Jane Cleland); Minden Pictures: 10 (Patricio
Robles Gil/Sierra Madre), 17 (Colin Monteath/Hedgehog House); NASA Earth Observatory: 4 (Reto
Stockli); Oxford Scientific: 3, 19 (Ann Eriksson/Nordicphotos)
Map: XNR Productions: 5

Library of Congress Cataloging-in-Publication Data
Ryan, Patrick, 1948–
  Welcome to India / by Patrick Ryan.
    p. cm. — (Welcome to the world)
  Includes index.
  ISBN-13: 978-1-59296-914-2 (library bound : alk. paper)
  ISBN-10: 1-59296-914-3 (library bound : alk. paper)
  1. India—Juvenile literature. I. Title.

DS407.R925 2007
954—dc22

2007005554

Contents

Where Is India?

Imagine looking at Earth from the moon. Most of what you see would be the blue oceans. The large areas of brown are called **continents.** There are seven of them. India is a diamond-shaped country that lies on the bottom of the continent of Asia. India is bordered by water on two sides— the Arabian Sea to the west and the Bay of Bengal to the east.

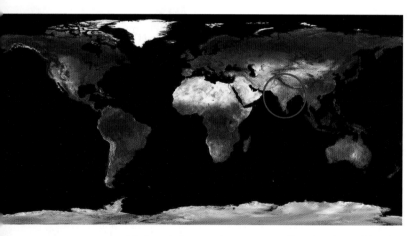

This picture gives us a flat look at Earth. India can be found inside the red circle.

Did you **know?**

India is made up of 28 states and 7 territories.

4

AFGHANISTAN

CHINA

INDIA
★ National capital
● Other city

Jammu and Kashmir

Himachal Pradesh

Arunachal Pradesh

PAKISTAN

Punjab
Chandigarh

Uttaranchal

Sikkim

BHUTAN

Haryana
Delhi

Delhi
★ New Delhi

NEPAL

Assam

Nagaland

Rajasthan

Uttar Pradesh
● Lucknow

Meghalaya

Manipur

Jaipur ●

Bihar

BANG.
Tripura

Mizoram

Gujarat
Ahmadabad ●

Madhya Pradesh

Jharkhand

Kolkata ●

MYANMAR
(BURMA)

Daman and Diu

Chhattisgarh

West Bengal

Dadra and
Nagar Haveli

● Mumbai

Maharashtra

Orissa

THAILAND

N
W ⊗ E
S

Hyderabad ●

Andhra Pradesh

Yanam ●
Puducherry

Bay of Bengal

Goa

Karnataka

Arabian Sea

Bengaluru ●

Chennai ●

Puducherry
Mahe ●

Puducherry

Puducherry

Tamil Nadu

Karaikal ●

0   150   300 miles
0   150   300 kilometers

Andaman and Nicobar Islands

Lakshadweep

Kerala

SRI LANKA

The Land

India is the seventh largest country in the world and contains many different land areas. The area in the southern part of the country is called the Deccan **Plateau.** A plateau is a land area that is higher than the areas of land around it. The Deccan Plateau is covered with flat plains. Along the coast of South India are mountain areas called the Eastern and Western Ghats. These are home to a rain forest and a large variety of animals and plants.

Many different kinds of plants can be found near the Western Ghats.

The northern part of India is covered with a mountain range called the Himalayas. *Himalaya* means "home of the snows." The tallest mountain in the world, Mount Everest, is in the Himalayas.

Most Indian rivers flow from the Himalayas when the snow melts in the summer. The most important of these rivers is the Ganges. It brings water to people, plants, and animals. Along the Ganges, rich farmland and rolling hills and plains can be found.

The Himalayas are the tallest mountains in the world.

Did you **know?**

India is the land of **monsoons**. Monsoons are ocean winds that often cause heavy rainfalls. The time of year when monsoons blow in is called the "rainy season." It begins in June and lasts several months. During one rainy season, an area of India can get up to 125 inches (317 centimeters) of rain! Children celebrate the rainy season by singing and dancing in the rain. The rain is also collected in large tanks to save it for the dry season.

The Ganges River has special meaning for people in India who belong to the Hindu religion.

7

Snow leopards live in India's mountains.

Plants and Animals

India is a land full of many beautiful animals. Elephants and many colorful birds, such as kingfishers, bee eaters, and sunbirds, can be found all over India. In the eastern part of the country there are rhinoceroses and wild buffaloes. Many monkeys, apes, leopards, and tigers live in special areas known as **sanctuaries** to protect them from being hunted. Snow leopards and mountain goats roam high in the Himalayas.

India's plant life is as varied as its animal life. In the north, trees such as evergreen, oak, and cedar grow. Bamboo and palm trees grow tall and thick in the southern parts of India. Sweet-smelling flowers and grasses of all kinds can also be found in India.

8

India has many tropical forests.

A farmer gets help from his animals to plow his land.

Long Ago

People have been living in India for thousands of years. The Indus Valley people were one of the first groups of people to live in India. They were followed by the *Aryans,* who divided themselves into different groups called **castes** (KASTS). In the caste system, people were born into jobs. If a child's father was a farmer, then the child would grow up to be a farmer, too.

Did you **know?**

The Aryans were an ancient people who came to what is now known as India more than 2,000 years ago.

For most of its history, India was made up of kingdoms with their own rulers. Then people from other countries took over the kingdoms. They made new rules for India's kingdoms and created new laws. The last country to rule India was Great Britain.

Mahatma Gandhi visits with his granddaughters.

India Today

About one hundred years ago, the people of India rose up. They did not want another country making laws for them. They wanted their own government with its own ideas. Many fights broke out between the British and Indian people. Great Britain did not want to give India up.

Then a peaceful man named Mahatma Gandhi spoke up. He wanted the fighting to stop. He used acts of non-violence to make the British people understand that India should be free. In 1947, India became a free country. Today, the people of India make their own laws to keep their people safe and happy.

Gandhi leads a march in 1947.

The People

India has the second largest population in the world—more than 1 billion people. Only the country of China has more people. Most of India's people are **descendants** of the Aryans or other groups that came to India long ago.

India's people work hard. They also like to spend time with their families and friends. Religion is also very important to many Indians. Many of India's holidays are religious celebrations.

Did you know?

With so many people in India, there are many who are poor and sick. In recent years, people have begun to help them. Mother Teresa was among those who fed India's poor and cleaned them. Today, other people carry on Mother Teresa's mission of caring.

A mother and son enjoy some time together.

People, cars, and other vehicles hurry about a busy street in New Delhi.

City Life and Country Life

Many Indians live in small villages and farm the land.

With so many people, India's cities are very crowded. Everywhere you look, there are people walking and talking. The bigger cities are full of busy streets and big buildings. There are shops and banks. There are hotels and restaurants, too. Most city dwellers live in tall apartment buildings.

Half of India's people are still farmers. They often live in small farming villages, in houses made from bricks or mud. In many of the houses, the only piece of furniture is a bed. During the day, they store the bed away so there is more room to cook and do chores.

Schools and Language

India is a land of many languages—hundreds of them are spoken throughout the country! The most common language is Hindi. English is also used as a common language by business people and government officials.

In schools, children are taught many of India's languages. They are also taught math, science, and the arts. Students study hard and like to learn. If they do well in school, Indian children can attend one of the country's fine colleges when they are older.

Did you know?

Lots of different languages are spoken in India, including Hindi, Urdu, and English. In fact, there are 22 national languages listed in the country's Constitution, or a written description of its government.

A group of schoolchildren from Chandigarh take a break from classes.

Work

Many Indians work as **traders.** They grow crops or make
things to sell to other countries. Cotton, peanuts, and rice are
all things that Indians produce for the trade business. Wheat,
milk, sugarcane, and rubber are important trade products,
too. India is also becoming known for its scientists. New
discoveries in medicine, electronics, and computers are
being made every day in India.

Tourism is another important business in India. In this job, Indians show visitors from other places about their country. Every year, many people come to India to see its fascinating sights.

One of the most famous tourist attractions is the Taj Mahal. It is a huge, beautiful building that was built almost three hundred years ago by a man named Shah Jahan. He made it as a tomb for his wife, Mumtaz Mahal.

Did you **know?**

It took 22 years to build the Taj Mahal.

21

An Indian family has lunch together at home.

Food

Spicy food is very popular in India. The most popular flavoring is a spice mixture called curry. Many Indians are **vegetarians,** which means they do not eat meat. Instead, they like to dine on lots of fruits and vegetables. Indians also like to eat dishes made with wheat and rice.

Chai tea is made from black tea and spices.

Sometimes a drink called lassi— a mixture of yogurt and water—is served with the meal. Indians also drink a dark tea called chai (CHAI).

Pastimes

Indian people love to go to movies. In fact, many large cities in India have hundreds of movie theaters! And hundreds of movies are made there each year. India is known for its movie musicals. Films are often filled with singing and dancing.

Since Great Britain ruled India for so many years, many of the sports that are popular in India are also popular British pastimes. Soccer, tennis, and field hockey are all favorite sports in India. Cricket is also popular with the Indian people. It is a game that is a little like American baseball.

Cricket is a popular game in India.

Movie posters let people know what's playing in their local theaters.

Holidays

Lots of holidays and festivals are celebrated in India. Since religion is an important part of India, many celebrations are religious. Holi is a celebration to mark the end of the cold season. Diwali is India's "Festival of Lights." Baisaki is the New Year celebration for India's Hindu religion. Muslims fast for a month as part of the holiday of Ramadan. Some Indians celebrate Christmas and Easter, just like many Americans.

Maybe one day you will get a chance to visit India. If you do, you might find it to be a very interesting country. You could enjoy one of the celebrations, see the Taj Mahal, try some spicy food, or even see an Indian movie. There are many different things to see and do in India!

A group of women light candles as part of celebrating Diwali.

Did you know?

Yoga originally came from India. Yoga is a series
of breathing exercises and body positions that
help people relax and remain fit.

Fast **Facts** About India

Area: 1,300,000 square miles (3,287,590 square kilometers)—about one-third of the United States.

Population: More than 1 billion people.

Capital City: New Delhi.

Other Important Cities: Mumbai (Bombay), Kolkata (Calcutta), Chennai (Madras), Bangaluru, Hyderabad, Jaipur, Ahmadahad, and Lucknow.

Money: The rupee.

National Language: Hindi. Many other languages are also spoken in India, including English.

National Holiday: Republic Day on January 26. Independence Day on August 15. Mahatma Gandhi's Birthday on October 2.

Head of Government: The prime minister of India.

Head of State: The president.

National Flag: Three stripes of orange, white, and green. In the middle of the white stripe, there is a blue wheel. The wheel stands for the laws people follow in their lives.

National Song: The national song of India is called "Jana-Gana-Mana."

> Thou art the ruler of the minds of all people,
> Thou Dispenser of India's destiny.
> Thy name rouses the hearts of Punjab, Sind,
>   Gujrat and Maratha,
> Of Dravid, Orissa and Bengal.
>
> It echoes in the hills of the Vindhyas and
>   Himalayas,
> Mingles in the music of Jamna and Ganges and
>   is chanted by
> the waves of the Indian sea.
> They pray for Thy blessings and sing thy
>   praise.
> The saving of all people waits in thy hand,
> Thou Dispenser of India's destiny,
> Victory, Victory, Victory to Thee.

Famous People:

Indira Gandhi: former prime minister, daughter of Jawaharlal Nehru

Mahatma Gandhi: a political leader involved in India's independence movement

Sunil Gavaskar: legendary cricket player

Lata Mangeshkar: singer

Jawaharlal Nehru: India's first prime minister

Aishwarya Rai: famous actress

Indian Recipe:

Sweet Lassi

One of India's tastiest drinks is also easy to make. Here's what you need:

2 cups plain yogurt
2 tablespoons sugar
4 ice cubes
½ cup of water
1 teaspoon lemon juice

Have an adult help you put all of the ingredients into a blender. Blend the mixture until it is smooth. This recipe makes enough for two servings. Feel free to add pieces of fruit, such as mango, into the mix for added flavor and sweetness.

How Do You Say...

ENGLISH	HINDI	HOW TO SAY IT
hello	namaste	nah-MUH-stay
goodbye	namaste	nah-MUH-stay
please	kripaya	KRI-pah-yah
thank you	dhanyavad	DHAN-yah-yaad
one	ak	EK
two	do	DOH
three	tin	TEEN
India	Bharat	BAH-rot

30

Glossary

castes (KASTS) Castes are different groups of people, traditionally divided by occupation.

continents (KON-tuh-nents) Most of the land areas on Earth are divided up into huge sections called continents. India is on the continent of Asia.

descendants (di-SEND-uhnts) People who come from a common ancestor, or relative, are called descendants. Children would be considered the descendants of their parents, grandparents, and earlier generations.

monsoons (mon-SOONZ) Monsoons are ocean winds that often cause heavy rainfalls. Monsoon season lasts several months in India.

plateau (pla-TOH) A plateau is an area of land that is higher than the land around it. The Deccan Plateau is a plateau in the southern part of India.

sanctuaries (SANK-choo-air-eez) Special places set aside for animals to protect them from hunters.

tourism (TOOR-iz-um) The business of showing travelers around a country is called tourism. Tourism is a growing business in India.

trader (TRAY-der) A person who grows crops or makes things to sell to other people or countries. Many Indians work in the trade business.

vegetarians (veg-uh-TAYR-ee-unz) Vegetarians are people who do not eat meat. Many Indians are vegetarians.

Further Information

Read It

Chatterjee, Manini, and Anita Roy. *India.* New York: Dorling Kindersley, 2002.

Das, Prodeepta. *Prita Goes to India.* New York: Frances Lincoln Children's Books, 2005.

Gassos, Dolores. *India.* Philadelphia, PA: Chelsea House Publishers, 2005.

Look It Up

Visit our Web page for lots of links about India:
http://www.childsworld.com/links

Note to Parents, Teachers, and Librarians: We routinely verify our Web links to make sure they are safe, active sites—so encourage your readers to check them out!

32

Index